CW01497471

# CLIFF AT 85

THERE'S NO STOPPING HIM

# CLIFF AT 85

## THERE'S NO STOPPING HIM

m
B

ICONS

Mirror Books

First published in hardback in Great Britain and Ireland
in 2025 by Mirror Books, a Reach PLC business.
www.mirrorbooks.co.uk
@TheMirrorBooks

ISBN: 9781917439312

Words by: Ashleigh Rainbird
Picture Editor: Natalie Jones
Lead Creative Designer: Chris Collins
Designer: Adam Ward
Picture Research: Holly Beckett and Lisa Tomkins
Picture Repro: Paul Mason
Chief Sub Editor: Roy Gilfoyle
Sub editors: Michael McGuinness & Lawrence Matheson
Commissioning Editor: Clare Fitzsimons
Operations Manager: Nick Moreton
Marketing and Communications Manager: Claire Brown

ISBN: 9781917439312

Printed and bound by Bell & Bain Ltd.
Glasgow G46 7UQ

# Contents

# CONGRAT

He is the legendary entertainer who has sold almost 300million records worldwide, landed 14 No.1s in the UK and is the only artist to reach top five in the album charts in eight different decades. There's no denying that, as Sir Cliff Richard reaches his 85th birthday, he has a lifetime of incredible accomplishments to celebrate.

Cliff's impact on the UK's music industry has been so significant, he became the first British musician to be knighted back in 1995, paving the way for so many of his contemporaries. It is just one of the many accolades he has collected during his much-lauded career, with two Ivor Novello awards and three Brit Awards to his name – with Lifetime Achievement honours dished out decades ago, when he was still only just getting started.

Since the teenage heartthrob achieved his first No.1 with Living Doll in 1959, his back catalogue of chart-toppers are an array of hits so well known that the entire country can sing along – 1962's The Young Ones, 1963's Summer Holiday and 1968's Congratulations to name just a few of his 14 multi-platinum selling hits to reach the top spot.

As he is proud to acknowledge, with 21.5million singles sold in the UK, the Official Charts Company revealed in 2012 that he was the third top-selling artist in the UK singles chart, beaten only by The Beatles and Elvis Presley. He is still the only UK act to have a No.1 single in five consecutive decades, having

>  **Cliff's impact has been so significant he became the first British musician to be knighted"**

topped the charts at least once between the 1950s-1990s.

In 2020, his album Music... The Air I Breathe cemented his run for having top 5 albums in the eight consecutive decades in which he became a TV, film and stage star in his own right, too.

It is no wonder fans in their thousands have gone to extreme lengths to see the star live.

In 1989, Cliff sold out Wembley Stadium twice, playing to a crowd of 144,000 across two nights for a pair of gigs during his From A Distance tour known as The Event, which went on to become a best-selling VHS and DVD. The same year, he released his 100th single, The Best Of Me – yet even better was to come.

As Cliff became a frequent performer at Britain's most prestigious events, including jubilee celebrations to mark anniversaries of

# ULATIONS!

Cheers! There have been plenty of reasons to celebrate during the eight decades of Cliff's career - he popped champagne when his hit We Don't Talk Anymore reached No. 1 in August 1979

**Photo credit:** Mike Maloney/Daily Mirror

Queen Elizabeth II's coronation and VE Day commemoration events, he also became a passionate philanthropist raising millions for charity via his Cliff Richard Charitable Trust, which he donated 10% of his earnings to. The Trust still raises around £500,000 for good causes every year. His unique ability to balance his rock 'n' roll superstardom with a devotion to his Christian faith came as a surprise to many, including the singer himself.

In 1998, Cliff started a record-breaking run that saw him sell out one of his favourite venues, the Royal Albert Hall, 32 times – fans camped out for a week for the opportunity to buy tickets, starting a trend for Cliff's most loyal supporters to pitch tents to ensure they could see their idol throughout his subsequent tours.

In March 1999, Cliff was presented with an award to mark his unique achievement at the historic venue – and his 2025 Can't Stop Me Now tour, which marks his 85th birthday, includes yet more performances at the Royal Albert Hall.

There really is no stopping the eternal Peter Pan of Pop.

03. A big milestone deserves a big cake – this one was presented to Cliff at Tower Records in London on 22nd July 1996 to celebrate 300,000 ticket sales for his Heathcliff musical

Photo credit: Alisdair MacDonald/Daily Mirror

02. Making waves: Cliff signalled to the crowd during the 50th anniversary of Cliff Richard and The Shadows with a performance at the the Metro Radio Arena, Newcastle, on 12th October 2009

Photo credit: Newcastle Chronicle & Journal

04. Puckering up, Cliff kisses the Lifetime Achievement Award he received at the 34th Ivor Novello Awards at London's Grosvenor House on 4th April 1989

Photo credit: Bill Rowntree/Daily Mirror

05.   Cliff showed off his famous hip-swinging during one of his earliest concerts at the Royal Albert Hall, alongside The Shadows on 18th September 1960

Photo credit: Bela Zola/Daily Mirror

06.   I do have the heart! He was given one of Variety Club's silver hearts for the top showbusiness personalities at a luncheon held at London's Savoy Hotel, alongside (L-R) Helen Shapiro and Rita Tushingham on 13th March 1962

Photo credit: Monte Fresco/Daily Mirror

**07** Fans enjoying Cliff's biggest concert The Event at Wembley Stadium, London, on 16th June 1989

**Photo credit:** Allen/Sunday People

08. Across two nights, Cliff entertained 144,000 fans at his The Event concerts at Wembley Stadium, pictured here on 16th June 1989

**Photo credit:** Daily Mirror

09. All aboard! The Summer Holiday star clambered aboard a familiar 1950s-style bus during Queen Elizabeth II's Platinum Jubilee Pageant in London on 5th June 2022

**Photo credit:** PA/Alamy

10. Jubilations! Cliff celebrated 25 years in the music business on 29th September 1983

Photo credit: Mike Maloney/Daily Mirror

11. Starry Knight: Sir Cliff Richard leaves Buckingham Palace after receiving his knighthood on 25th October 1995

Photo credit: Kent Gavin/Daily Mirror

# THE YOUNG ONE:
## Cliff's early years

> "As tough as those times were, my sisters and I had no memory of being unhappy"

**H**e has one of the most recognisable names in rock 'n' roll history, but the man who would become Cliff Richard was born Harry Rodger Webb, on 14th October 1940 in the King's English Hospital in Lucknow, India.

His dad Rodger worked at a catering firm on the railways, which afforded Cliff and his younger sisters an affluent lifestyle during their early years – the family had servants and were comfortably well-off at their home in Howrah, close to Calcutta. Cliff idolised his father, who helped inspire his love of music as he played banjo in a jazz band. Though he was a passionate musician himself, Rodger could have had no idea he would one day go on to help manage his superstar son's lucrative career.

In 1948, Rodger and his wife Dorothy, Cliff's mum, decided to relocate back to the UK where they had family, amid growing racial tensions after Britain granted India independence. At the time, seven-year-old Cliff was one of three siblings, with two younger sisters Donna and Jacqueline - and moving a family of five halfway around the world was understandably expensive. Rodger was forced to sell the majority of the family's possessions

to fund their three-week-long expedition via the SS Ranchi steamliner – a journey that left Cliff, especially, seasick. They arrived at Tilbury Docks in Essex at 6am on 13th September 1948, with Rodger having just £5 left to his name. With no alternative accommodation available, the Webbs had to move in with their grandmother Dorothy and her seven children in a three bedroom, semi-detached house in Surrey – it was a huge change to their privileged lifestyle in India. With Cliff accustomed to eating curry every day, British cuisine came as a culture shock, too, and he recalled to Desert Island Discs in 2020: "I can remember three main meals a week were a soup bowl with two slices of toast with tea poured over it. Milky tea and sugar sprinkles on it." But while they might have been on the breadline, Cliff has predominantly fond memories of his "poverty-stricken" childhood. "As tough as those times were, my sisters and I had no memory of being

01 Wonderful to be young! Harry Webb as a toddler in India, before his family brought him to the UK

Photo credit: Moviestore/Shutterstock

unhappy," he told the Daily Mail in 2017. Yet the lack of wealth inspired Cliff to become ambitious, and as a youngster he promised his mum he would one day buy the family a house – it was a promise he make good even sooner than he could have imagined.

During primary school, the change in environment was tough on Cliff. Not only was Britain lots colder – the youngster had never seen snow, and was fascinated when he first saw a winter's frozen flakes – his different upbringing was apparent to his classmates, and he was bullied at his Surrey school where he was cruelly nicknamed "Indi-bum". Though Cliff gave back as much as he got – he boasts he never lost a single fight at school, and was even able to draw blood with his punches. "I was always in battles on the playground," he confirmed to Piers Morgan's Life Stories in 2020 – but chuckled as he clarified he has not been involved in any fisticuffs since.

Playground life improved when the family moved into an aunt's home in Waltham Cross, Hertfordshire, yet their financial struggles remained – the Webb family had now expanded to six, welcoming Cliff's baby sister Joan. All six slept in a single room together, until finally securing a three-bedroom council house to call home in 1951: 12 Hargreaves Close in Cheshunt. The house now features a plaque celebrating the star's humble beginnings – and he returned to the Bury Green Estate for a nostalgic tour in 2020, where he pointed out a cupboard he used to sleep inside. His parents Rodger and Dorothy slept on a mattress on the floor, as the family were too poor to buy any furniture, until Rodger found work as a clerk at electrical firm Atlas Lamps. There, Rodger acquired some wooden crates from deliveries, and carved out furniture for the family. With grit and determination, their hard graft was paying off and the family's living conditions were steadily improving – Rodger's pride and drive gave root to his son's strong-minded work ethic that would stay with him throughout his career successes. "My parents brought me up to respect things and it kept my feet on the ground," he explained to the Daily Mail in 2020.

By the age of 12, Cliff had already set his sights high – and wrote to a pal that his ambition was "to be a famous singer". His talents shone from an early age as he attended an after-school drama club. His favourite teacher Jay Norris cast him as Ratty in a 1955 production of Toad of Toad Hall, and encouraged him to perform his first solo song on stage – reluctantly, he agreed, and was surprised to discover how much he enjoyed the experience; his passion for performing was born. Cliff always remembered how Jay had

>
> **My parents brought me up to respect things and it kept my feet on the ground"**

*02.* *All shook up… Elvis obsessive Cliff, pictured in 1958, practised his idol's lip curls in the mirror and recreated his iconic quiff with Brylcreem*

**Photo credit:** Daily Mirror

*03.* *The Webb family travelled for three weeks on board the SS Ranchi steamliner while moving to the UK from India*

**Photo credit:** Alamy

04. *Keeping it in the family: Cliff with (L-R) a family friend, dad Rodger, mum Dorothy and to his right, his then manager Ray Mackender in Chelsea, London in 1958*

Photo credit: Alamy

05. *Dad Rodger, who bought his son's first guitar, watches admiringly as Cliff strums on stage in New York in January 1960*

Photo credit: Daily Mirror

inspired him, and he invited her to see him perform at the Royal Albert Hall in 2020 as a guest of honour, when she was 100 years old, telling the Daily Mail: "Without Jay Norris, I would never have known I could sing."

However, his love for music was truly sparked aged 15, the very first time he heard the song Heartbreak Hotel by Elvis Presley playing from a car radio – the memory is so significant, he can even recall the make of car, a dark green Citroen, and that it was May 1956. It was this very moment he decided to become a rock 'n' roll star: "That's the reason why I've followed my dreams," he said of the momentous occasion on Desert Island Discs in 2020. Cliff immediately became enamoured with his idol, saving up his pocket money to buy records, replicating his idol's famous quiff hairstyle with Brylcreem and practising his impressions of Elvis' trademark snarl and knee jerks in his bedroom mirror. It wasn't long before he formed a band with his school friends, the

pop and doo-wop group The Quintones, which enabled him to show off his new moves on stage. For his sixteenth birthday, dad Rodger bought him his first guitar and taught him how to play his first few chords, which he would practise in front of the mirror. "It made me feel the way I thought rock and rollers should look and feel," he told Desert Island Discs.

By his own admission, music became an obsession, particularly the music of Elvis. Speaking to the Daily Mirror in 1959, an 18-years-young Cliff was proud to say: "Rock 'n' roll is my life. I idolise Elvis Presley; I even dream about him." He took a job at a potato farm to save up enough money to buy records, but also got into trouble at school for skipping class to buy tickets for a Bill Haley concert. He blames his preoccupation with music for hindering his academic efforts, after he failed all his O-Levels besides English Language. But by the age of 17, while working with his dad at the electrical shop, Cliff formed another band with his friends Terry Smart and Norman Mitham, which they called The Drifters. Their second ever gig at the Five Horseshoes in Hoddesdon was attended by sewage lorry driver John Foster who saw their potential and promised them that with his management, he could make them stars. And the rest is history.

# I'M *NEARLY* FAMOUS

**T**hanks to their new manager, John Foster, The Drifters performed their first London gig at the 2i's in bustling Soho - they played for a week for 10 shillings (50p) each. There, they met concert promoter Harry Greatorex, who invited them to perform at his venue, the Regal Ballroom in Ripley, Derbyshire – but Harry would have a lasting effect on the group.

It was the promoter who first decided the group should be billed as "Harry Webb and The Drifters", singling the frontman out in keeping with a trend, thanks to bands such as Bill Hayley & his Comets and Buddy Holly & The Crickets. But the band feared "Harry Webb" did not sound very rock 'n' roll. To concoct a new name for their lead singer, they retreated to nearby Soho pub the Swiss Tavern, where suggestions included Russ Clifford, and Cliff Russard, before they eventually decided upon Cliff Richard. With a cliff face being made of rock, they reasoned it certainly sounded rockier than Harry, plus his new surname was reminiscent of Little Richard. New Drifters bandmate Ian Samwell also suggested that the name would be more memorable as Cliff would be forced to correct anybody who mistakenly called him Cliff Richards – they wanted to make sure their frontman stuck in everyone's minds. Cliff immediately requested that his family and friends call him by his new, cooler name. "I went into that pub Harry Webb and I came out Cliff Richard," he laughed on Desert Island Discs. On 3rd May 1958, Cliff Richard and The Drifters gave their debut performance in an hour long set in Ripley, during which they covered Elvis - and the crowd loved them. Within a month, girls were screaming his name – and soon after, he was chased down the street in Shepherd's Bush. "It was my first taste of being a real rock and roll star," he recalls in his 2020 memoirs, The Dreamer. "I loved it

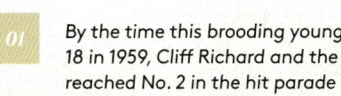

By the time this brooding young star turned 18 in 1959, Cliff Richard and the Drifters had reached No. 2 in the hit parade with *Move It*

**Photo credit:** Terry Fincher/Daily Herald

more than I had ever loved anything before."

With momentum building, the band recorded a demo, and were quickly signed up by Columbia. While preparing to record their debut single, Drifters member Ian Samwell penned a new, original song, Move It, while riding a bus on his way to meet the group for rehearsals. They knew instinctively they had a hit. Move It had been due to be the B-side to their cover of Schoolboy Crush when it was released in August 1958, but was flipped to be the main single within a month when it gained traction – and it gained traction quickly; Cliff recalls leaping up and down with his family in Cheshunt when it was first played on BBC Radio. Before long, it was racing up the charts, and the group were invited to perform on ITV's Oh Boy!. Cliff spent his first pay cheque from the single – £60 – on a TV for his parents, so they could watch the group's television debut on 13th September 1958, in front of an audience of around 7.2 million. The producer of the TV show, Jack Good, moulded Cliff into a pop star, advising him to look less like an Elvis tribute act, and how to command a stage and perform for cameras. "I thought something could be done with this boy," Jack told the BBC in 1981. "There was magic in his eyes." Jack also taught him how to smoulder for the cameras – and the girls in the audience went wild. Speaking to the Daily Mail in 2017, Cliff said: "I believe I am what I am today because Jack got me thinking of how I should present myself: as me and not just a reflection of someone else."

He certainly made his mark. The group continued to go down a storm, and returned to perform on the show weekly. Move It became a No. 2 chart hit – kept off the top spot by Connie Francis's Stupid Cupid – and Cliff celebrated in Cheshunt once more. "I think the echoes of my sisters' and my mum's screams of joy can still be heard there...," he laughed to the Manchester Evening News in 2021. "And I got a hug from my Dad!" Cliff was becoming a standout star, with girls chasing him in the

02  Cliff Richard and the Drifters, as they were known in 1959 (L-R): Hank Marvin, Tony Meehan, frontman Cliff and Bruce Welch

Photo credit: Beverly Lebarrow/Redferns/ Getty

street as well as screaming throughout his performances. Asked what his secret was, in attracting such devoted fans, he told the Daily Mirror in 1959: "I do things with my face. What gets 'em is when I get carried away in a sort of agony... I can tremble my bottom lip. Did it by accident on television, and the girls went mad." His hip shakes were also causing a stir, as he added: "I wiggle. Everybody wiggles in rock 'n' roll." On his 18th birthday in 1958, he performed with The Drifters in Leicester, where the crowd sang Happy Birthday and threw presents on stage – by this point, the up-and-coming group, which now featured Hank Marvin, Jet Harris and Bruce Welch, were outshining the headline act The Kalin Twins.

Their phenomenal success crossed the Atlantic, too, and amid potential legal issues with a US band called The Drifters, the group were forced to change their name, and opted for Cliff Richard and The Shadows – with Jet Harris and Hank Marvin reasoning, only slightly jokingly, that the band members were always in Cliff's shadow. But the group were of course popular in their own right, and in 1960 the Shadows' instrumental single Apache knocked Cliff Richard and the Shadows' single Please Don't Tease off the top spot in the Hit Parade. A "bittersweet" moment, Cliff described in his autobiography The Dreamer.

In 1960, just four years after he first heard Elvis Presley, Cliff had become dubbed the "English Elvis" and was a superstar in his own right. Before he even turned 20, he was able to spend £7,000 (the equivalent of £210,000 today) purchasing a five bedroom semi-detached house in Winchmore Hill, North London in March 1960 for his whole family to live in. He swelled with pride at being able to treat his family, having since told his friend Gloria Hunniford on the Biography Channel: "When you're a child and sitting on your mum's knee, you say: 'One day I'm going to buy you a house.' Well, I did!'" He had asked Rodger whether he should buy a house or a car first, and plumped for the house – but also managed to afford a grey Sunbeam Alpine that became his pride and joy. The significant purchases

**"** I believe I am what I am today because Jack got me thinking of how I should present myself: as me and not just a reflection of someone else"

came just a year after he told the Daily Mirror his ambition was to make enough money to buy his parents a house, to star in films and to get a Gold Disc. By 1962, with gold discs aplenty, Cliff Richard and the Shadows were given an Ivor Novello award for Outstanding Service to British Music and his family were settled in their new homes. The Box Office had beckoned him, too.

*03.* *Cliff while chatting to Donald Zec from the Daily Mirror at his home in Radford Road in Coventry, Warwickshire in April 1959*

Photo credit: Bill Ellman/Daily Mirror

04 The Drifters became regulars on ITV's Oh Boy! as their debut single Move It raced up the charts, seen performing on 25th January 1959

**Photo credit:** Bob Hope/Daily Mirror

*05* *Thirsty work... Cliff sips a drink while judging the Girls and Boys Talent Exhibition at London's Earl's Court on 18th August 1959*

**Photo credit:** Terry Fincher/Daily Herald

07

08

06. Cliff's Drifters became his Shadows - always in his shadow, they joked - when the group performed at London's Prince of Wales Theatre on 29th July 1962

Photo credit: Mirrorpix

07. Off to the Big Apple! Posing by a jet engine at London Airport, now Heathrow, back in January 1960, before heading to New York, where he later moved

Photo credit: Arthur Greated/Daily Mirror

08. No. 1! As Living Doll topped the hit parade, a delighted Cliff signed autographs for fans while filming Expresso Bongo on 27th July 1959

Photo credit: George Greenwell/Daily Mirror

09. *Me and my Shadows… Cliff Richard and The Shadows backstage at The Regal, Cambridge on 10th November 1959 (L-R) Jet Harris, Bruce Welch, Tony Meehan and Hank Marvin*

Photo credit: Cambridge News

10. Cliff proudly shows off the home he bought for his parents in Winchmore Hill, North London in March 1960, achieving a childhood ambition

———————
Photo credit: Carl Bruin/Sunday Pictorial

11. He could also already afford to buy his first car - a grey Sunbeam Alpine fitted with red leather interiors, which became his pride and joy

———————
Photo credit: Carl Bruin/Sunday Pictorial

The crooner shows off the come-to-bed eyes that made girls scream as he strips out of a pair of striped pyjamas while showing off the family's new Winchmore Hill home

**Photo credit:** Geoffrey Day/Daily Mirror

13. And the award goes to... Cliff and the Shadows received the Outstanding Service to British Music at the 7th Ivor Novello Awards in London on 13th May 1962

14. A new Shadow! Debuted at EMI on 3rd November 1963, John Rostill (right) became Cliff's new bandmate after Brian "Licorice" Locking left the group to focus on practising as a Jehovah's Witness. Licorice had previously replaced Jet Harris in the group

15. Ready for a Summer Holiday? Cliff and co. recorded Bachelor Boy and Big News at London's Abbey Wood Studios London on the 20th November 1962

Photo credit: Albert McCabe/Daily Express

16. That's Liza-with-a-Z! Cliff and pal Liza Minelli - then just 18 - lark about on a flight of steps on 17th June 1964, while rehearsing for an ATV special Cliff And The Shadows

Photo credit: Brian Randle/Daily Herald

17. Cheers! The Shadows celebrate as their instrumental single Apache reaches the top spot - knocking Please Don't Tease by Cliff Richard and The Shadows into No. 2 on 18th August 1960 (L-R) Cliff Richard, Tony Meehan, Hank Marvin, Jet Harris and Bruce Welch

Photo credit: Bela Zola/Daily Mirror

18. A decade of those coveted Golden Discs. The group celebrated their 10th anniversary at a party in London on 26th September 1968 (L-R) John Rostill, Cliff, Hank Marvin, Brian Bennett and Bruce Welch

Photo credit: Newcastle Chronicle & Journal

19. He was already a Credit to Showbusiness in 1966, and was named as such by Radio Luxembourg at their luncheon on 14th December 1966

Photo credit: Mirrorpix

20. By the turn of the 1970s, Cliff was experimenting with new style - and new career prospects...

Photo credit: Shutterstock

18

19

20

01. *Hot Property indeed! A floppy-haired Cliff braves fans in Birmingham on 13th June 1973 to film Hot Property, also known as Take Me High*

**Photo credit:** Dick Williams/Daily Mirror

# HOLLYWOOD *IS* CALLING

**C**liff was cast perfectly as an up-and-coming rock 'n' roll singer in his first major motion picture role in 1959's Serious Charge.

Though he had little acting experience – besides his solo singing performance as Ratty – he landed the role of Curley Thompson alongside Anthony Quayle and Winston Churchill's daughter Sarah. While he enjoyed the experience, he grumbled that he had to sit in makeup every morning having his hair permed, to fit the role of the character "Curley". The role saw him perform Living Doll, written by Lionel Bart, which Cliff personally did not like – speaking in 1998, Cliff recalled "passionately refusing" to record the track for release. But once Drifters bandmate Bruce Welch suggested performing the track in a country style, they started to warm to it. The new version went on to become the biggest-selling record of 1959 with 770,000 sales, and more than a million worldwide, earning Cliff his first much-coveted gold disc – he achieved his ambitions to land a gold disc and a part in a film at the same time!

Serious Charge opened him up to a wider audience and paved the way for Cliff's burgeoning film career. Later in 1959, Cliff was cast as Bert Rudge, or Bongo Herbert, in Expresso Bongo – a risque film that saw his young rock 'n' roll singer character seduced by an aging American starlet Dixie Collins, played by Yolande Donlan. Until now, the billing on both films' credits had been "introducing Cliff Richard" – but that all changed once he signed up as the top-billed star in The Young Ones in 1961. The film's most famous scene sees him perform an enthusiastic vaudeville routine to What D'You Know, We've Got A Show, when the characters have broken into a rundown theatre they club together to try to save. But while the

 **I looked in the mirror, checked back on some of my old pictures and had to admit she was right. It was a truth I couldn't ignore"**

scene was lauded, it is remembered by Cliff for the wrong reasons – seeing himself on the silver screen sparked a lifelong commitment to dieting, as he felt unhappy with his weight. He was horrified when he was referred to as "that chubby Cliff Richard" on Coronation Street by Minnie Caldwell. "My first reaction was 'Me? But I'm the British Elvis'," he laughed, speaking in 2013. He told the Daily Mail: "I looked in the mirror, checked back on some of my old pictures and had to admit she was right. It was a truth I couldn't ignore." After gorging on fatty food during his US tour with the Shadows, he went on a strict diet, cutting down to one meal a day and dropped from 12 stone 7 lbs to 10 stone, just in time for his Summer Holiday.

Again, the star was to receive top billing on the credits in the 1963 film, which saw him play a young mechanic who rents a London Transport double-decker red bus and travels around Europe with his friends in it on holiday. He spent six weeks filming in Greece alongside Una Stubbs and Lauri Peters, and said making

the project was just as fun off-screen as the characters have on it. "Once shooting got under way, there was an amazing buzz," he told the Daily Mail in 2013. "Summer Holiday really was more like a holiday than work. I swanned around Greece for six weeks on a red London double-decker bus with a group of good mates and we were all paid for the privilege." The film produced hits including Summer Holiday and Bachelor Boy, and even prior to its release it had made an impact. At the premiere in Leicester Square, Cliff arrived by limousine, with plans for the cast to travel around the square on a double-decker bus. But more than 3,000 fans had turned up, with girls hammering on his car window as he attempted to reach the Warner Theatre, prompting police to order him to drive away. The singer was frustrated as it meant he missed his own premiere and he went home to his manager's house and watched the event on TV instead.

It would not be his only stint filming abroad. In 1964, he relocated to the Canary Islands

*02.* *Take Me High jinx! Cliff shoots his final movie role in Hot Property/Take Me High alongside cast members Anthony Andrews, from Brideshead Revisited, and Ben Hur's Hugh Griffiths on 19th June 1973 in Shelswell Park, Oxfordshire*

Photo credit: Coventry Evening Telegraph

for three months to film Wonderful Life, his co-star Susan Hampshire remembered holding hands in some of their romance scenes. She told the Daily Telegraph in 2007: "I remember thinking: 'Gosh, what lovely skin. These are the most exquisite hands I've ever touched.'" The pair had to dance on sand dunes, which they found tricky to adapt to after learning choreography in a studio in London. Wonderful Life was not as well received, and went over budget due to rain on location – as Cliff has bluntly put it: "Wonderful Life was a flop. It was a disaster from the word go." But that did not deter him from making more films, and two years later he starred in Finders Keepers alongside Viviane Ventura – though sadly for the star, this time, the Spanish setting was recreated in Pinewood Studios. He transferred his acting skills to the stage, appearing opposite Una Stubbs again at the London Palladium's pantomime of Aladdin and his Wonderful Lamp in 1964, and starring in Five Finger Exercise in the New Theatre in Bromley, Kent in 1970. However, Cliff has admitted feeling in a "lull" of movies and despite returning to the big screen in 1973's Take Me High, a Birmingham-based musical which was also known as Hot Property, he felt the huge successes he achieved with Summer Holiday and The Young Ones were never quite matched. Take Me High, in which he played a merchant banker tasked with helping a struggling restaurant, was his final film.

## 03

04

03. A Serious star: the young actor's first film role was alongside Andrew Ray (right) in 1959's Serious Charge, where Cliff was appropriately cast as an up-and-coming rock 'n' roll singer called Curley

**Photo credit:** Moviestore/Shutterstock

04. The roles kept coming, and Cliff starred in Expresso Bongo, in the main role as a naive singer Bongo Herbert, with scenes set in Soho striptease bars

**Photo credit:** George Konig/Shutterstock

05.    In Expresso Bongo, Cliff's character Bongo
       Herbert is seduced by an older American
       starlet played by a sequin-clad Yolande
       Donlan. The pair filmed together on set on
       27th July 1959

Photo credit: George Greenwell/Daily Mirror

06. What a side kick! Actress Carole Gray played
Cliff's girlfriend Toni in *The Young Ones*, with
scenes set at the fictional Countess Theatre
shot at London's Finsbury Park Empire on
28th July 1961

**Photo credit:** Freddie Reed/Daily Mirror

07. *The Young Ones'* famous Vaudeville routine
features Cliff alongside Teddy Green in
scenes recorded at London's Abbey Road on
2nd August 1961

**Photo credit:** Daily Express

08. On the buses! Cliff and the Shadows pose with a London Transport double-decker bus - but plans to attend the Summer Holiday premiere on Leicester Square on 10th January 1963 were thwarted by enthusiastic fans

**Photo credit:** Arthur Sidey/Daily Mirror

09. Dancing Shoes! Cliff and his Summer Holiday co-star Lauri Peters had a spring in their step as they practiced their routines while filming together at Elstree, Hertordshire on 15th May 1962

**Photo credit:** Malcolm McNeill/Daily Mirror

10. Ready for her close up... Clearly a talent behind the camera too, Cliff spent his 23rd birthday on set of Wonderful Life with Susan Hampshire on 14th October 1963

**Photo credit:** Bela Zola/Daily Mirror

09

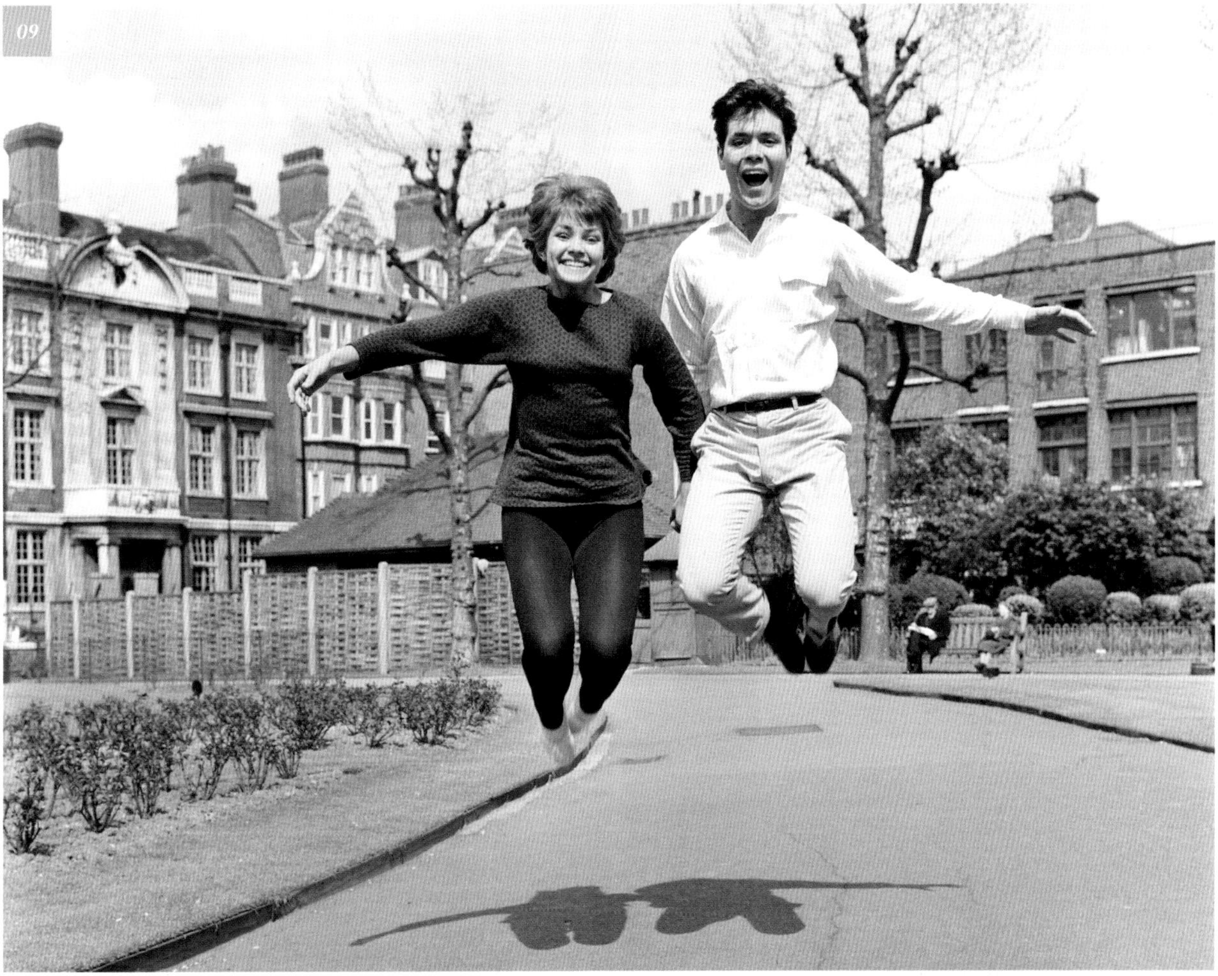

10

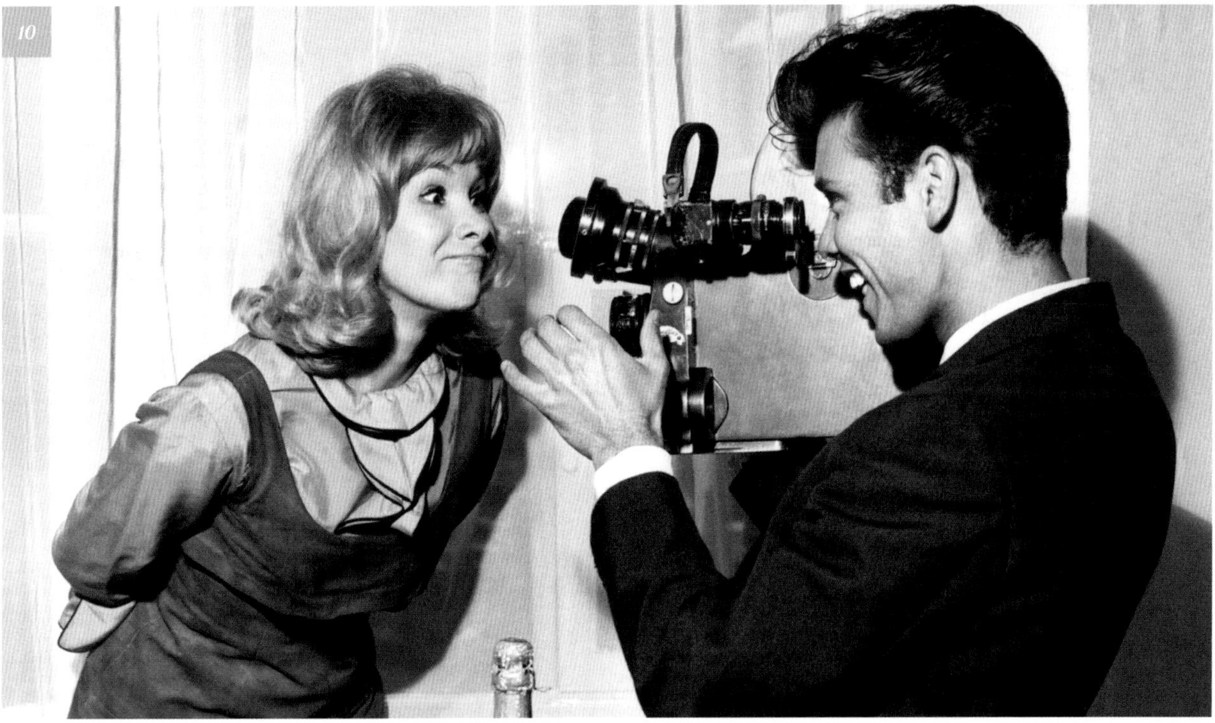

11. *On The Beach! Cliff and co-star Susan Hampshire had to perform dance routines on Canary Island beaches for Wonderful Life, filmed in November 1963*

**Photo credit: Mirrorpix**

*12.* Oh Senorita! Colombian actress Viviane
Ventura was cast alongside Cliff in Finders
Keepers in June 1966 - the same summer she
was England's official mascot for the World
Cup winning side

**Photo credit: Mirrorpix**

13. *Time Drags By… Cliff and The Shadows enjoy a break from filming Finders Keepers with co-star Viviane Ventura at Pinewood Studios on 20th June 1966*

**Photo credit:** Larry Ellis/Daily Express

14. *Kiss! Combining his love of film with religious projects in Billy Graham's Two a Penny, Cliff puckered up with Ann Holloway in scenes shot on 5th July 1967*

**Photo credit:** Daily Mirror

15. With Deborah Watling, who later became a Doctor Who assistant, filming Take Me High at the Birmingham Strathallan Hotel on 3rd June 1973

Photo credit: Birmingham Post and Mail

16. The pair messed around on a riverboat while filming the movie, also known as Hot Property, in Wootton Wawen in Warwickshire on 7th June 1973

Photo credit: Birmingham Post and Mail

*01* *Faithful One: becoming Christian led to the rock 'n' roll star performing to the congregation at the Queen's Road Baptist Church in Coventry on 7th March 1971*

**Photo credit:** Coventry Evening Telegraph

# A LEAP OF FAITH:
## Cliff becomes a Christian

**W**hile Cliff recited prayers before every meal and attended church weekly during his childhood, he did not feel particularly religious growing up – he even declined to be confirmed at the age of 14. But after his beloved dad Rodger's death from complications caused by thrombosis, aged just 56 on 15th May, 1961, Cliff started to bring a copy of the Bible with him on tour, and began reading verses as his father had once encouraged him to do when he was younger.

It was also through his grief that he first considered joining the Jehovah's Witness religion. While touring Australia in the months after his dad's death, he suggested to bandmate Brian "Licorice" Locking that he might consult a medium to try to contact his father beyond the grave. Licorice, a devoted Jehovah's Witness, reacted angrily, and quoted from the Bible to warn him off the idea, sparking an interest in Cliff. As he discussed it with more friends, his former teacher Jay Norris introduced him to Bill Latham, a religious education teacher at Cliff's old school, who then invited him to attend Christian Bible study classes. Through their friendship, Cliff became increasingly confident that Christianity was his path. He looked up to his Christian friends' "purposeful and fulfilled" lifestyles, and felt that before he found God he was "dangling around" as a singer. "It led to me committing my life to Jesus," he says.

Cliff has often cited the Bible verse that convinced him Christianity was his calling, Revelation 3:20: "Behold, I stand at the door and knock. If any man hears my voice and

 *I didn't have anyone to turn to the way I can talk to God. I said 'Please, come into my life. Change me'"*

opens the door, I will come in to him, and will sup with him, and he with me." He can pinpoint the moment he decided to become a Christian, and recalls sitting on a bed in Bill's home where he was temporarily residing while filming Finders Keepers. "I said to myself, 'Okay, make the change in me'," he said in an ITV documentary. "I didn't have anyone to turn to the way I can talk to God. I sat at the end of my bed and I said: 'Please, come into my life. Change me.'"

Quietly, he started practising the religion from 1964, before going public with his beliefs on 16th June 1966, at the Reverend Billy Graham's Greater London Crusade rally. Despite warnings he could lose fans over the decision, with one peer cautioning he could be about to commit "professional suicide", a headstrong Cliff opted to face his fears and talk about finding God in front of 27,000 people at Earl's Court. Speaking at the lectern, he praised his parents for bringing him up on the Bible and told the crowd: "I can only say to people who are not Christians that until you have taken the step of asking Christ into your life, your life is not worthwhile. It works. It works for me." He performed a cover of No Secret, a gospel song that was also recorded by Elvis. "It was a terrifying moment for me," he told Desert Island Discs. "I was so scared. But it did lead to me beginning to be able to speak the name Jesus without feeling embarrassed."

The announcement came as a shock to many, but Cliff approached his faith with the same tenacity he utilised in becoming a successful rock and roll star. Within a month of the Billy Graham rally, Cliff called a press conference to announce that he would essentially retire from the showbiz spotlight to focus on becoming a teacher of Christianity. He studied for an O-Level in religious education

in Lewes, East Sussex but instead chose to pursue new showbiz opportunities that incorporated his faith. He would later describe this choice as his "little Isaac", comparing his decision to not sacrifice his career for God to the Bible story about Abraham being willing to sacrifice his son Isaac, as per God's test. "Of course, I got terrible press: 'We knew he was kidding!' this sort of thing," he shrugged while speaking to the Church of England newspaper. "But at least I'd made a stand."

It was to be the star's mission to combine being a pop star and a Christian, having proved to himself that the two most important elements of his life did not need to be mutually exclusive. He found he could include his faith within various aspects of his career, including recording his gospel album Good News in 1967. That same year, he starred in the Billy Graham

02

Organisation's film Two a Penny, playing a drug-dealing, misguided youth whose girlfriend has a spiritual awakening at one of the preacher's crusades. He refused to accept a fee, donating it straight back to the organisation. He finally decided to be confirmed in the religion shortly before Christmas that year, by the Bishop of Willesden at St Paul's Church in Finchley, North London. Two years later, he starred in a six-part religious series for Tyne Tees TV called Life With Johnny, which retold Christian parables, featuring his friend Una Stubbs as part of a star-studded cast. It was also in 1966 that the singer set up the Cliff Richard Charitable Trust, which cemented his lifelong passion for philanthropy. Throughout his career, he has donated 10% of his income to charitable causes. Yet Cliff has cited how it took seven years for him to be fully convinced that he made the right

decision by staying in showbusiness. In 1973, he visited Bangladesh with The Evangelical Alliance Relief Fund (TEAR Fund), a Christian charity that aims to tackle poverty. Realising he was not cut out to administer injections, a nurse advised him to fundraise as his way of helping – and he has gone on to raise hundreds of thousands for the charity alone. In his autobiography he writes: "I have absolutely no doubt that it is the most important thing that I have done in my entire life."

02.  Cliff's first public appearance as a Christian was at a "crusade" held by The Reverend Billy Graham at London's Earl's Court on 16th June 1966

**Photo credit:** Daily Mirror

03.  The American evangelist preacher's visit to the UK was highly publicised thanks to Cliff's attendance

**Photo credit:** John Downing/Daily Express

Addressing rally attendees on 16th
June 1966, Cliff announced that he was
"proud" to declare himself a Christian

**Photo credit:** Blandford/Daily Herald

05. *Speaking after his June 1966 appearance Cliff said he felt on "a tremendous high" to be able to speak freely about his faith and had been "terrified" he might lose fans*

**Photo credit:** Blandford/Daily Herald

06. *Some fans reportedly wept following his revelation, fearing he would quit rock 'n' roll – but it sparked an ambition to incorporate his faith into his career*

**Photo credit:** Blandford/Daily Herald

07. *Cliff signs copies of David Winter's biography of him New Singer, New Song, which documented his conversion to Christianity in October 1967*

**Photo credit:** Mirrorpix

08. *Billy Graham visits Cliff and Dora Bryan on the set of religious film Two a Penny in June 1967*

**Photo credit:** Mirrorpix

09. *After releasing a gospel album, Cliff performed at the Jesus Festival in Hyde Park, London on 1st September 1972*

Photo credit: John Cleave/Daily Mirror

10. The event was part of the nationwide Festival of Light, where Cliff sang to a crowd of 50,000 Christians amid protests outside

Photo credit: John Cleave/Daily Mirror

11. Cliff and Billy Graham were joined by fellow rocker Johnny Cash at another Christian festival, the Spree at London's Wembley Arena on 1st September 1973

Photo credit: Sunday Mirror

# ROCK

**01** *"The Peter Pan of Pop" appeared ageless while performing at his From A Distance tour in Birmingham on 1st November 1990*

**Photo credit:** Adam Fox/Birmingham Post and Mail

# 'N' ROLL JUVENILE:

## Cliff's balance of rock 'n' roll and Christianity

Cliff's career was going from strength to strength as he reshaped his image. Yet now he had embraced Christianity, he feared he would be considered a "wimpy, Bible-bashing goody two shoes".

So it was a bold decision to represent the UK at the 1968 Eurovision Song Contest, as the competition was regarded by many as being naff. But the public got behind the song Congratulations when Cliff performed against six different contenders on the BBC – and he looked almost certain to claim victory on the night, before Spain's entry, La La La by Massiel, caused a shocking upset by pipping him to the win by a single point. It is a result that still stings Cliff to this day, with him openly stating on multiple occasions that he was "robbed". There have since been claims that Fascist dictator General Franco bribed Eurovision juries for the victory. "If there is evidence that I was the winner, there won't be a happier person on the planet," Cliff told the Guardian. He later represented the UK again at the competition in 1973 with Power to All Our Friends, when he came third. Sadly, he said in 2023 that he would be unlikely to enter again.

Remarkably, he managed to maintain his role as both a Christian and a rock 'n' roll star throughout the Swingin' Sixties, where hippy culture was thriving and the Beatles, and their fondness for hallucinogens, were making waves worldwide. Cliff, on the contrary, embraced becoming a clean, family entertainer. He would later remark that he simply felt he had nothing to rebel against, though his decision to go against the tide could be deemed an act of rebellion in itself. But Cliff did fall briefly out of fashion during the glam rock era of the 1970s. As Bill Latham explained: "There was a downturn in his career after the arrival of other artists who eclipsed him." Undeterred, Cliff undertook the challenge of reinventing himself, which prompted yet another era from the star that would defy his critics.

In 1976, he released Devil Woman from his album I'm Nearly Famous, and immediately regained his cool – though he quipped to Piers Morgan's Life Stories: "I always thought I was cool!" However, he did initially air concerns about the song's title and meaning, due to its connotations of the devil conflicting with his faith. He decided to rework the lyrics to something he was personally happy with prior to recording the track. In 1992 he told Cross Rhythms: "I turned it from a guy who got involved with the occult. I added things like 'stay away', 'beware the Devil woman', 'she's gonna get you', 'you'd better get out of there fast.' By doing that it became a warning against the occult." With rave reviews and commercial success, it would also become Cliff's biggest hit in the US, and he wrote in his autobiography that his resurgence was "a comeback beyond my wildest dreams".

In 1982, he managed to release another album of gospel songs, Now You See Me, Now You Don't, without alerting his record label to it being gospel – a hoodwink he is still thrilled with. Indeed, in the 1980s, the singer demonstrated a unique ability to combine all his passions without compromising his music credentials; his Comic Relief re-record of Living Doll with comedy group the Young Ones topped the charts and proved the singer still had a great sense of humour, all while his incredible charitable trust fundraising facilitated him in fulfilling his Christian mission. He told TV Times: "I've always maintained I'm the most radical rock 'n' roll singer Britain has ever seen. I was the only one who didn't spit or swear or sleep around. I didn't do drugs. I didn't get drunk. I didn't indulge in soulless sex. And I've always felt comfortable with the decisions I've taken. I like being Cliff Richard." His army of devoted fans has always liked him just the way he is, too.

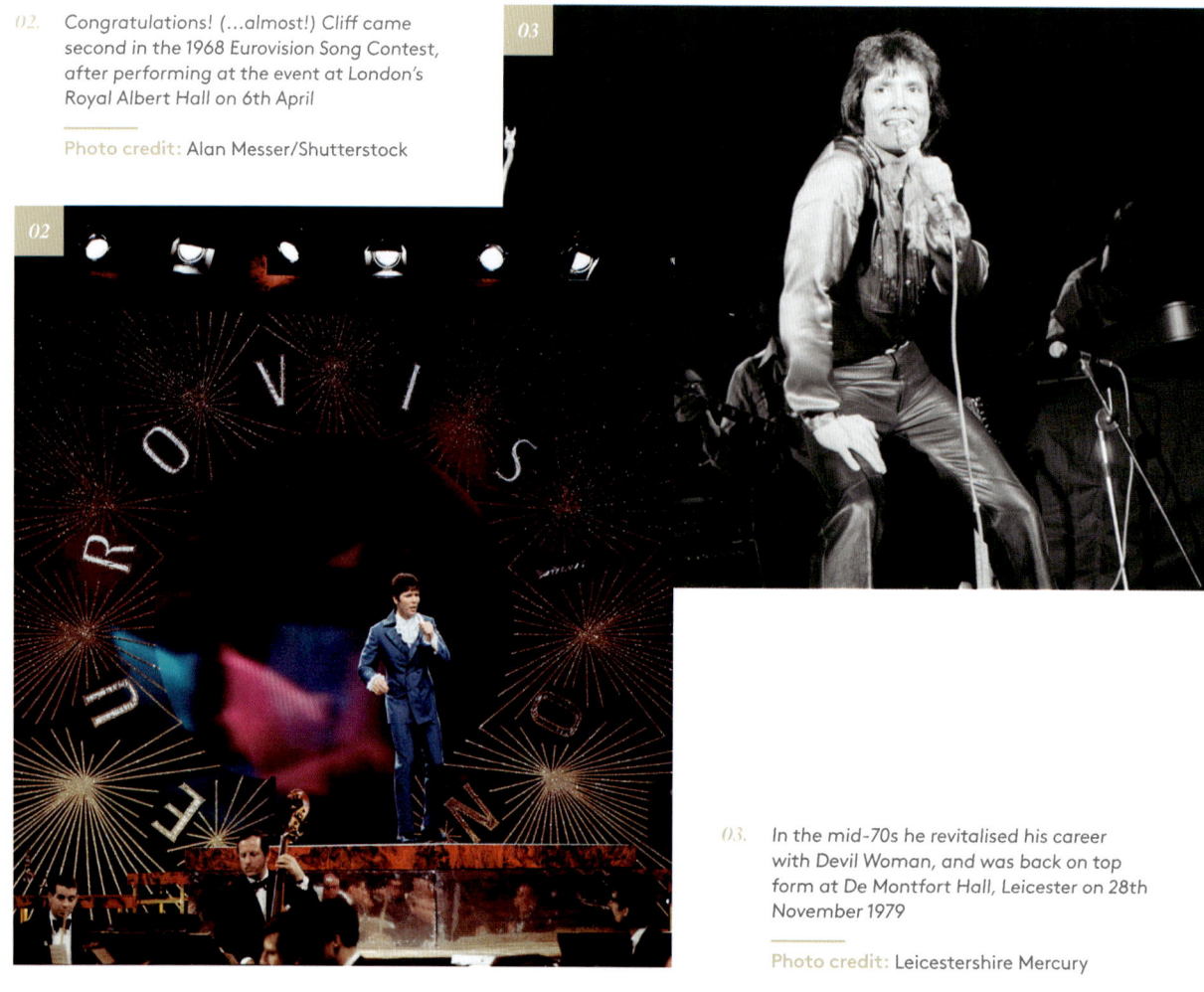

02. Congratulations! (...almost!) Cliff came second in the 1968 Eurovision Song Contest, after performing at the event at London's Royal Albert Hall on 6th April

Photo credit: Alan Messer/Shutterstock

03. In the mid-70s he revitalised his career with Devil Woman, and was back on top form at De Montfort Hall, Leicester on 28th November 1979

Photo credit: Leicestershire Mercury

04. *Wowing students at Binley Park School, Coventry on 12th November 1976, he was always accumulating new fans*

Photo credit: Coventry Telegraph Archive

05. Cliff fused pop with gospel in the 80s, which went down well with the crowd at the Montreux Golden Rose Pop Festival on 11th May 1984

Photo credit: Bill Rowntree/Daily Mirror

06. Turning his attention to the stage, he starred alongside Dawn Hope, Jodie Wilson and Maria Ventua in the musical Time at the Dominion Theatre, pictured on 25th March 1986

Photo credit: Bill Rowntree/Daily Mirror

07. Former drummer Dave Clark, pictured with Cliff on 26th July 1985, wrote the stage show Time and personally asked him to star in it

Photo credit: Kent Gavin/Daily Mirror

08 *Cliff continued speaking at preacher Billy Graham's rallies including at the Mission England Crusade at Villa Park, Birmingham on 6th July 1984*

**Photo credit:** Birmingham Post and Mail

*10. Cliff gamely re-recorded Living Doll with the cast of TV series The Young Ones for Comic Relief on 28th April 1986*

Photo credit: Comic Relief/Comic Relief via Getty Images

The singer gave an interview to the *Daily Express* in church while promoting his album *Always Guaranteed* on 29th July 1987

Photo credit: Michael Dunlea/Daily Express

12. In another church interview, Cliff
spoke to the Rector of St Martin in the
Bull Ring in Birmingham, Rev John
Wesson on 10th December 1987

Photo credit: Birmingham Post and Mail

13. *Heathcliff… it's me! Fascinated by Emily Brontë's Wuthering Heights character Heathcliff, the singer created and starred in his own musical about the brooding anti-hero*

**Photo credit:** Roger Allen/Daily Mirror

14. *Wearing a dark wig with sideburns, he portrayed the tortured soul at Heathcliff's premiere at the National Indoor Arena in Birmingham on 12th November 1996*

Photo credit: Roger Allen/Daily Mirror

15. *Cliff continued speaking about his faith into the 90s including at St. Martin in the Bull Ring in Birmingham on 9th November 1990*

**Photo credit:** Andrew Fox/Birmingham Post and Mail

16. *He never stopped performing - seen here with his guitar on 28th June 1995 - despite becoming a fig farmer in Portugal in the 90s. Multi-talented!*

**Photo credit:** Julian Brown/Sunday People

01. Action! Cliff and his Shadows were as comfortable behind the camera as they were in front of it - larking about with equipment in Blackpool on 23rd August 1963 (L-R Brian "Liquorice" Locking, Brian Bennett, Cliff, Hank Marvin and Bruce Welch)

Photo credit: Daily Mirror

# THE CLIFF RICHARD SHOW:

## Cliff's life on screen

**W**hile Oh Boy!'s Jack Good was delighted with Cliff's first television appearances, and fans were going wild for his hip shaking, not everybody was quite so taken with their first taste of Cliff on the box in the 1950s...

The NME considered the star "too sexy" for British TV with one reviewer scoffing that his "hip-swinging was revolting, and not the sort of performance any parent would want their child to witness". The BBC even gave internal guidance to camera operators to only film him from waist height to avoid his controversial hips, reportedly as "his movements are too explicit and morally questionable for family viewing". He recalled being known as a "crude exhibitionist" while being interviewed by BBC's Michael Parkinson. But at the time, Cliff shrugged off such accusations: "If people say I'm too sexy in my singing, that's it – I can't help it. I don't push it, believe me. I just get carried away. I do exactly what the songs tell me inside I gotta do."

It quickly transpired that Cliff was definitely not too sexy for the screen, as his TV career proved to be another lucratively successful arm for the singer – pretty soon he had become a

 **Suddenly I wasn't just this pop rock singer. I was having to do skits and sketches on television and I loved it"**

hit on the small screen in his own right. He became the titular star of his own Associated Television (ATV), now ITV, variety show The Cliff Richard Show in 1960. An offshoot of Val Parnell's Saturday Spectacular, it saw him perform his own tracks as well as covers alongside the Shadows, but also diversify into different types of entertainment by dressing up as Tarzan alongside Barbara Windsor. "Suddenly, I wasn't just this pop rock singer," Cliff recalled to Iain Dale, speaking on stage at the Hammersmith Apollo. "I was having to do skits and sketches on television, and I loved it."

The audience loved it, too, and the following year, he was commissioned for an extended series, this time simply titled Cliff.

In 1970, his most famous TV series, It's Cliff Richard, aired on the BBC, featuring songs, comedy sketches and huge star guests including Aretha Franklin. It also platformed the performances that were competing to be the Eurovision Song Contest's British entry in A Song For Europe. The popular series continued for four years, cementing him as a true star of Saturday night TV. Guests included his friends, and co-stars Una Stubbs and Hank Marvin made regular appearances during the run,

before in 1976 it was revamped with tweaks to the format and retitled It's Cliff Richard and Friends.

Along the way Cliff has clocked up 160 appearances on Top of the Pops – more than any other artist. The latter stat, Cliff joked in his autobiography, is "probably because I'm older than everyone!" After the 1970s, Cliff largely starred in one-off specials, such as on The Hit List, and over the years, he has also been the subject of multiple documentaries and chat show specials to mark his various milestones in showbiz. He continues to be a ratings success story, regardless of the format he puts his name to.

02

01

Me Tarzan, you Cliff! For a spoof of *Expresso Bongo*, Cliff portrayed a jungle boy raised by Tarzan (Mario Fabrizi) alongside Barbara Windsor. The skit was for the singer's first run of hour-long TV specials *The Cliff Richard Show*, as part of Val Parnell's *Saturday Spectacular*, filmed at the Edgewarebury Country Club at Elstree, Hertfordshire on 8th July 1960

Photo credit: Daily Mirror

03 ▶ 04

03. Tin man! Cliff appeared on ATV's Tin Pan Alley TV series in 1960

**Photo credit:** ITV/Shutterstock

04. Throughout the 1960s, more shows were commissioned by the ATV network including the 1965 series Cliff Richard and the Shadows (L-R): John Rostill, Bruce Welch, Hank Marvin, Cliff and Brian Bennett

**Photo credit:** ITV/Shutterstock

05. The group also starred on other variety programmes, including The Billy Cotton Band Show filmed for the BBC on 28th August 1962

**Photo credit:** NCJ Archive

06. By Royal appointment... In October 1962, they also performed for Queen Elizabeth II during the Royal Command Performance at the London Palladium

**Photo credit:** Mirrorpix

07. Cliff was starstruck to perform alongside Judy Garland's then-17-year-old daughter Liza Minnelli on ATV's Cliff Richard and The Shadows on 17th June 1964

Photo credit: Mirrorpix

08. Not such a diamond geezer: he also played burglar Riley Walker opposite Marian Diamonds as Maggie Brown in the TV play A Matter Of Diamonds in February 1968

Photo credit: Bella Zola/Daily Mirror

## 08

09. *Cliff managed to combine his Christian values with his TV career as he starred opposite actress Cindy Kent in Tyne Tees Television's Life for Johnny on 8th January 1969*

Photo credit: Daily Herald

11.  Cliff cracks a joke and makes Mike Yarwood
     giggle while recording his Thames TV
     Christmas show on 11th December 1984

     **Photo credit:** Peter Case/Daily Mirror

12.  The star celebrated 30 years of his career
     with Terry Wogan on a special edition of the
     Wogan show on 16th April 1988

     **Photo credit:** Daily Mirror

13. Collaborating with crooner Michael Ball on ITV's *The Michael Ball Show* in 1993

Photo credit: ITV/Shutterstock

14. Cliff and The Shadows' final TV performance coincided with their 50th anniversary tour on *The Paul O'Grady Show* on 30th November 2009

Photo credit: ITV/Shutterstock

15 · *The singer spoke about his childhood and visited an early home on Piers Morgan's Life Stories TV Show on 25th October 2020*

**Photo credit:** ITV/Kieron McCarron/ Shutterstock

# CLIFF

01 *You're My World: Cliff wears synchronised sequins with Cilla Black on stage at Wembley Arena during his From A Distance tour on 7th January 1991*

**Photo credit:** Chris Wood/Daily Express

# *and* FRIENDS

**D**uring his eight decades in showbiz, Sir Cliff Richard has accumulated a collection of A-listers as his best friends.

His close relationship with the late Cilla Black started way back in the mid-1960s, when the pair met during numerous appearances on the BBC's weekly music programme, Top Of The Pops, and he found she could always make him smile and laugh. Their friendship became even closer when they both moved to Barbados – though he joked to the Daily Mail that he was her unofficial "chauffeur" on the Caribbean island, and later described how he ferried her around in a Dukes of Hazard-style vehicle, with the pair finding it hysterical to see her clamber out of it. Cilla, in turn, considered Cliff part of her family, describing him as being a "very close friend for a million years" while supporting him through a difficult period in his life. He sang a poignant rendition of Faithful One in memory of his beloved pal at her funeral in 2015, when he told the crowds she was "the greatest TV presenter of all time", and said tearfully: "I know all of our souls will be united together. Cilla, this is just a hiccup in our relationship and we'll see you again and I'm looking forward to that time."

Actress Olivia Newton-John met the star in the 1970s when she was dating Shadows member Bruce Welch, and went on to accompany Cliff as a backing singer on tour. She then starred as a regular on his TV show, It's Cliff Richard which catapulted her

> **Cilla considered Cliff part of her family, describing him as 'a very close friend for a million years'"**

to fame and she went on to star in Grease. The pair collaborated on several songs, including Suddenly from her 1988 film Xanadu, and went on to become firm friends, though only ever platonic. He described her as his "soulmate" who he "loved" when she died aged 73 from breast cancer, and said: "She remains very much alive."

Holiday presenter Jill Dando was a Cliff Richard "superfan" before the pair met, and they became such close friends he had been due to lend her his Rolls Royce to use on her wedding day. Tragically, she was murdered in 1999 before her dream ceremony could take place. He said in an ITV documentary to remember the late star on the 20th anniversary of her murder that he always feels how one of his "closest friends" is missing in her absence. A friendship with Gloria Hunniford blossomed from the early 1970s, when she interviewed him for Radio Ulster, and to this day, he considers her "one of my best friends in the world," after

*Cliff first met Cilla Black backstage at Top of the Pops in the mid-sixties - she perched on his knee for a photo in March 1968*

**Photo credit:** Tom King/Daily Mirror

her support throughout his more difficult times.

Cliff also impressed some of the finest musicians in the world. A quote the singer treasures came from the late Beatles star John Lennon, who once opined: "Before Cliff and Move It there was nothing worth listening to in British music." Cliff describes the praise from the legendary star as "an honour I will take to my grave". A friendly rivalry between the Beatles and Cliff and the Shadows saw them bicker over their respective popularities. Cliff reportedly once scoffed: "Their name just sounds like something you tread on!"

In scenes reminiscent of Cliff's attempts to replicate Elvis, Queen frontman Freddie Mercury honed his own performance skills by doing impressions of Cliff in the mirror, as

his bandmate Roger Taylor has confirmed, while Sir Brian May agrees Cliff "inspired" the flamboyant frontman.

His close friend Dame Shirley Bassey performed at his 60th birthday, and Sir Elton John affectionately calls his friend by several nicknames, 'Sylvia Disc' – as he was apparently always so keen for receiving Silver Discs. Elton, who gifted Cliff a gold Cartier watch after their 1986 collaboration on Slow Rivers, also described him as 'the Bionic Christian', due to his ageless looks. But it is all in good humour, with Elton, Jimmy Page and Elizabeth Taylor all helping to promote Cliff's 1975 album by wearing I'm Nearly Famous badges. He revealed in 2020 that he had recorded a version of We'll Meet Again with the late Dame Vera Lynn, which he still hopes to release.

03. A winning trio at the Disc and Music Echo Valentine Pop Poll Awards on 13th February 1970 at London's Cafe Royal, where Cilla (left) was named top British singer, Cliff was named Mr Valentine and singer Lulu (right) was given the Miss Valentine honour

Photo credit: Eric Harlow/Daily Mirror

04. Anyone Who Had A Heart: Cliff and Cilla both shared a passion for philanthropy, and she celebrated at his Wembley concert where £120,000 was donated on 7th January 1991

Photo credit: Chris Wood/Daily Express

05. The pair often supported their celebrity friends, teaming up to cheer on Joan Collins at her first night performing in the Over The Moon play, and partying afterwards at the Waldorf hotel on 15th October 2001

Photo credit: OK!/Mirrorpix

*06.* You're The One That I Want: Cliff considered Olivia Newton-John, pictured here with him in May 1983, to be his "soulmate"

**Photo credit:** Mirrorpix

*07.* The pair met in the early 1970s, and her career took off thanks to her appearances on The Cliff Richard Show at the London Palladium, this picture taken on 11th October 1971

**Photo credit:** Bela Zola/Daily Mirror

*08.* Hopelessly Devoted: Their inseparable bond saw them perform together throughout the decades, including at the Monaco Pop Festival on the 8th May 1992

**Photo credit:** Mirrorpix

09. With another close friend, TV presenter Gloria Hunniford, who he also met in the early 70s, at the Hampton Court Flower Show on 5th July 1999

**Photo credit:** Alisdair MacDonald/Mirrorpix

10. His strongest supporter. Cliff and Gloria walked the red carpet together at the Daily Mirror's Pride of Britain Awards on 31st October 2016

**Photo credit:** Phil Harris/Daily Mirror

11. Cheers! Clinking glasses with Dame Vera Lynn at Buckingham Palace for the 50th VE Day Commemorations on 8th May 1995

**Photo credit:** Tony Weaver/Daily Express

12. Happy 21st! In July 1979, Cliff was joined by (L-R) Anita Harris, Elaine Paige, Joan Collins and Patti Boulaye to celebrate his 21 years in showbusiness

**Photo credit:** Mirrorpix

13. Cliff and Queen frontman Freddie
Mercury hung out backstage at a
party for Time musical's Dave Clark
at London's Dominion Theatre on
16th December 1987

Photo credit: Daily Express

14. A star man: Cliff rubbed shoulders
with David Bowie at the Disc and
Music Echo Valentine Pop Poll
Awards at the Cafe Royal in London
on 13th February 1970

Photo credit: Eric Harlow/Daily
Mirror

*15.* *Cliff helped dry his close friend Jill Dando's feet after she cooled them in a pool at the Hampton Court Flower Show on 8th July 1997*

**Photo credit:** Alisdair MacDonald/Mirrorpix

16.  *He teasingly calls him Sylvia Disc and the Bionic Christian, but Sir Elton John has been a great friend of Cliff's for many years, with the pair pictured together at the Nordoff Robbins Music Therapy Concert at Knebworth in 1990*

**Photo credit:** Richard Young/Shutterstock

# FAMILY MAN

**C**liff was fortunate enough to always be enshrouded with the love of a close knit family who would have supported him whatever his career choice might have been.

His rise to fame almost took a different turn thanks to his mother Dorothy, who enthusiastically posted an application for her son to appear on Hughie Green's TV talent show Opportunity Knocks in 1956. Alas, it would not be Cliff's path – and while dad Rodger wanted Cliff to ensure he always had a back-up plan, Dorothy persisted in her encouragement for him to pursue his music ambitions.

Cliff's three sisters, Jacqui, Donna and Joan, were also rocks to the fledgling star, so it was a very proud young man who bought their first family home in Winchmore Hill in 1960. He also managed to persuade both his parents to stop working by the time he was 20, as he was able to provide for the whole Webb family. It was still just 12 years after they had arrived in the country with £5 to their name.

It was a remarkable achievement, but wealth was never Cliff's parents' priority, and Rodger – a "strong role model" for his son, who ruled the house firmly, according to Cliff – in particular felt his son was unhealthily overworked. In 1958, he was alarmed to see his son lose his voice while juggling early call times for filming Serious Charge, with television appearances on Oh Boy! and a Finsbury Park residence every night in the same week, and sacked his management team – including John Foster, who had first discovered the Drifters. The overwhelming demands of showbusiness had taken their toll so much that at the time, Cliff told Dorothy he may quit the industry for good. Rodger saw that his subsequent management contract stipulated designated time off for his son.

 **While I think I would have been a good father, I've given myself to my family and wouldn't have it any other way"**

## 01

A Forever Kind of Love: Cliff was a doting son to his mum Dorothy Webb, who he hugged at the launch of his album Always Guaranteed on 27th August 1987

**Photo credit:** Bill Rowntree/ Daily Mirror

It was, tragically, a timely intervention. Over Christmas in 1960, Rodger, a heavy smoker, was hospitalised with heart problems and given just four and a half months to live. In his final days, he restructured Cliff's management team once more, recruiting Peter Gormley to head up operations in March 1961. Cliff was still only 20 when Rodger died in May that year, aged just 56.

Cliff immediately committed to his role as man of the house and took his responsibilities as a breadwinner seriously. But he began to find the negative impact of his fame on his family difficult, and was devastated when his sister Donna's 1961 wedding descended into chaos, despite police cordons in place at the venue, Waltham Abbey church. In 1963, he paid £11,000 for a seven-bedroom Tudor-style mansion called Rookswood, in Upper Nazeing, Essex, to live in with Dorothy and his two younger sisters, Jacqui and Joan. The new family home was far more secure, sitting among 11 acres and with plenty of garage space for Cliff's growing car collection!

The family remained close, and Cliff and his sisters were a supportive network while his mum struggled with a 10-year battle with dementia prior to her death in 2007, aged 87.

He was devastated by the loss of sister Donna after a long illness in 2016, aged 73. Jacqui and Joan have spent large portions of time during the subsequent years with Cliff at a vineyard in Portugal and at home in Barbados with him.

Speaking about his decision not to marry or start his own family in 2013, he said it had "never bothered" him – especially as mum Dorothy already had 11 grandchildren. "My three sisters have children, and it's been wonderful to watch them grow up, get married and start families of their own," he told The Lady. "I've made sure I've always played a part in their lives. So while I think I would have been a good father, I've given myself to my family and I wouldn't have it any other way."

"I like my life," he told Michael Parkinson. "I have a really perfect life."

02.   Aged 20, Cliff took his family to Spain for the Christmas holidays, seen here with sisters Joan, 10, left, and Jacqueline, 13, and mother, Dorothy Webb at Heathrow Airport on 12th December 1960

Photo credit: Alamy

02

04. Cliff with mum Dorothy at their Cheshunt council home in 1959, just as his career was taking off

Photo credit: Alamy

03. Dorothy kissed her son goodbye at London Airport, now Gatwick, as he and the Shadows set off to tour South Africa on 12th January 1963

Photo credit: Dove/Daily Express

The proud star bought his family a six-bedroom mansion at Upper Nazeing, Essex where he and mum Dorothy, and sisters Jackie, then 16, and Joan, 13, lived from 10th November 1963

**Photo credit:** Arthur Sidey/Daily Mirror

06 Cliff said he loved spending time at Rookswood with his mum and "kid sisters", at the Essex home, after sister Donna had moved out of the family home to get married two years earlier

**Photo credit:** Mirrorpix

07. Cliff gave his sister Joan away at her wedding to Colin Phipps in Hoddesdon, Hertfordshire on the 9th March 1968

Photo credit: Daily Express

08. Dorothy accompanied Cliff to the Eurovision Song Contest in Luxembourg, where he placed third. They are seen returning home on 8th April 1973

Photo credit: Victor Crawshaw/Daily Mirror

09. Stand by for action! Cliff attended the Thunderbirds Are Go premiere at the London Pavilion on 12th December 1966 with family (L-R): former chauffeur Derek Bodkin, who wed Cliff's mum Dorothy, beside him, in 1966, several years after Rodger's death. Cliff's sister Donna is on the right

Photo credit: Daily Mirror

10. We are family: Cliff shares a squeeze with sisters Joan (left) and Jacqui (right) at a 50th anniversary lunch thrown in his honour by Variety at the Dorchester Hotel Ballroom Park Lane on 19th September 2008

Photo credit: Alan Davidson/Shutterstock

*11.* *Fields of Gold: his passion for wine led to him buying a winery in Adega Do Cantor in Guia, Algarve, Portugal, where he is pictured on the 12th July 2012*

**Photo credit:** Alamy

# BACHELOR BOY

**T**hanks partly to his 1963 Summer Holiday hit of the same name, Cliff's reluctance to wed earned him the reputation of being a Bachelor Boy. However, the Man of Mystery singer has repeatedly said he prefers to be known as more of an "enigma" – though has openly discussed past relationships, revealing there are two women he came extremely close to marrying.

His first girlfriend was former schoolfriend Janice Berry in 1957, but when Cliff saw heartbroken fans stamping on his posters because they saw he had a girlfriend, he broke up with her in 1958 to focus on his career. It was an early sign of things to come for the headstrong star.

Around 1960, he had a tryst with Brigitte Bardot-like Carol Costa, who had been married but was in the process of separating from his bandmate Jet Harris. Cliff broke off the relationship immediately after his mum discovered love letters between them, and voiced her upset about the relationship, and on multiple occasions since, Cliff has said he considers their romance to have been a mistake.

In 1960, he dated Delia Wicks, but broke up via a letter while on tour in Australia. In the letter, which became public after her death in 2010, Cliff, then 21, wrote he felt "confused" about their relationship, and added: "Being a pop singer I have to give up one very priceless thing – the right to have any lasting relationship with any special girl." Shortly after Delia, he fell for dancer Jackie Irving, the first woman he considered marrying. However, a manager warned marriage could cost him a third of his fanbase, which made it out of the question for Cliff! He has lamented in his later years that times have changed considerably for modern pop singers.

Cliff broke up with Jackie – who went on to marry musician Adam Faith – while he was filming Wonderful Life in the Canaries, alongside co-star Una Stubbs. He was also linked to Una at the time, and speaking to Piers Morgan, he confirmed the pair, who went on to feature together many times, were "romantically involved".

Despite his public romances, Cliff was persistently the subject of rumours regarding his sexuality, including over his relationship with Bill Latham who lived with him in

*01* Oh no he didn't! Cliff says he was never romantically involved with his Aladdin and Wonderful Lamp co-star Una Stubbs, pictured at the London Palladium on 17th December 1964

Photo credit: Arthur Sidey/
Daily Mirror

Weybridge, Surrey, until 1996, when Bill moved out to live with his wife. Una was one of many of Cliff's flames who spoke out against the rumours, telling The South Bank Show in 1993: "There have always been suggestions that he's homosexual... The fact is, he isn't."

Cliff also dated tennis player Sue Barker, who he met at a Shadows concert in 1981. While he "seriously contemplated" proposing to Sue, he lamented to the Daily Mail: "I realised that I didn't love her quite enough to commit the rest of my life to her." Sue later said the pair had fallen out over him saying several similar sentences in other interviews.

Still, gossipers persisted, and he wrote with frustration in his 2008 memoirs, My Life, My Way, that he was "sick to death" of the rumours about his sexuality that still plagued him. He went on to speak candidly in the book about his friendship with former priest John McElynn, who he describes as a "companion".

He explained the pair live together because "I don't like living alone". Again, as recently as 2020, he was asked about his sexuality and simply said he preferred to be known as an enigma.

He added that there was little chance he would marry after he turned 80 – fittingly for a man whose love of music has dominated his life, he is still a bachelor boy like in one of his most famous melodies, and that's the way he is very likely to stay.

04. *Cliff's The Shadows bandmate Jet Harris'
former wife Carol Costa, pictured on 8th
June 1964*

Photo credit: Evening News/Shutterstock

05. *Cliff considered marrying Sue Barker, who
celebrated his 25th anniversary as a star
with a special Variety Club lunch on 8th
December 1983*

Photo credit: Mike Maloney/Daily Mirror

*Serving up an ace! Cliff plays tennis at the Hurlingham Club in July 1994*

**Photo credit:** Steve Wood/Daily Express

# ANYONE FOR TENNIS?

**C**liff is as much of a staple at the Wimbledon tennis championships as strawberries and cream and Pimm's, attending all 14 days of the 2025 tournament in an array of snazzy blazers. For decades, he has insisted the fortnight of the championships is clear in his diary, and thanks to a rather memorable occasion in 1996, he will forever be associated with the tournament – and its rain!

But his love for tennis – which developed over the years, helped in part by his Rookswood home having its own court – turned into a passion for the sport when he met Sue Barker in 1981. The pair had initially bonded over their shared religious beliefs, but Cliff was thrilled when she invited him for a match, a match in which Cliff laughs in his The Dreamer memoirs that if she had played a proper game: "I would have been lucky to get love."

In 1990 he played another female tennis champ, Steffi Graf and recalls how she moved around the court "like a blur". A moment of triumph that he is still delighted by happened during a charity tennis tournament in Australia, when he aced pro player Amélie Mauresmo – a "fluke", he insists.

In 1991, he set up the Cliff Richard Tennis Development Trust, with pros taking on celebs at the event in Brighton to raise money for charity. It was such a success, it ran for two decades and featured A-list stars including Sue, Elton John, Terry Wogan and Barbara Windsor. He was already synonymous with the sport and in 1993, when he bought his vineyard in Portugal, his love of tennis was so integral to his life that he incorporated nets into a coat of arms that sat above his Quinto do Moinho winery.

But in 1996, one of his compulsory days off to attend Wimbledon created a moment he will always be remembered for. As the SW19 courts had become famous for, rain stopped play – on 3rd July, it rained for three hours, leaving the crowd restless and bored. Cliff was summoned by the All English Tennis Club, and agreed to go on to court and give an interview, but the journalist pressed him to give the crowd a song. He chose to sing an uplifting acapella rendition of Summer Holiday to lift the mood amid the unending rain. He then asked the crowd: "Do you remember the Young Ones?" After launching into that, a collective of tennis champs including Pam Shriver and Martina Navratilova joined him on court for Bachelor Boy. "I never thought I'd play the Centre Court," he remarked in awe to the crowd, later joking that he brought his own racket.

Still a devoted tennis fan, in 2008, he said he still plays the sport for at least an hour every day, and told Lorraine's Ross King in 2017 that he hopes to still play when he is 100.

02. Watching the Wimbledon tennis championship with former girlfriend Sue Barker leaning in for a cuddle in June 1982

**Photo credit:** Jack Kay/Daily Express

03. Now an annual visitor, Cliff wore a pastel suit to Wimbledon on 4th July 2016 - and gives the crowds a cheerful wave

**Photo credit:** Phil Harris/Daily Mirror

04. The singer's famous performance on Centre Court to entertain the rain-sodden crowds on 3rd July 1996, which saw him joined by tennis stars

Photo credit: Mirrorpix

05. He returned to Centre Court to repeat his performance for the 100th anniversary celebrations of the Wimbledon championships on 3rd July 2022

Photo credit: Tim Merry/Daily Star

06. Cliff's love of tennis combined with his passion for philanthropy, and on 25th September 1985 he joined children at Bisham Abbey, Berkshire competing in his search for a new tennis star

Photo credit: Richard Reed/Daily Mirror

07. He started a series of celebrity tennis tournaments, and was joined by stars and pro-players including (L-R) Hank Marvin, Annabel Croft, Shakin Stevens, Sara Gomer and Mike Read on 21st December 1985 at the Brighton Conference Centre

Photo credit: Allen Olley/Daily Mirror

*A real honour! One of the star's proudest achievements was receiving his knighthood from the Queen on 25th October 1995*

**Photo credit:**
Bob Barclay/Daily Express

# *ARISE* SIR CLIFF

" **When the Queen came to me with the sword I was a nervous wreck. Had my dad been there it would have been fantastic"**

appear at the event throughout the decades, until he sang for Prince Charles and Camilla in 2008.

His closest royal friend was the "very kind" Princess Diana, who "impressed" him with how down-to-earth she was. Once, after sitting beside the star at dinner, she requested a pair of marigold gloves from the hosts, so she could help wash up in the kitchen. "I thought it was terrific," Cliff laughed to The Reverend Canon Roger Royle. "I didn't think any of the royals would know what marigold gloves were!" He and Diana both shared a love of tennis, and the singer told Lorraine's Ross King that he would often be at the same ski resort in Lech, Austria with Diana and Charles and they would all end up singing together at the hotel bar. Princes William and Harry even sang holding chocolate bars as pretend microphones one evening, Cliff recalled. He was one of few entertainers who were invited to attend

B y 1995, Cliff had become a staple performer at some of the UK's largest celebrations often attended by the royals – that year alone he had a leading role at the 50th anniversary of D-Day events, prior to receiving what would become one of his proudest achievements, a knighthood.

But Cliff's friendship with the royals started when he first performed in front of the Queen Mother at the 1959 Royal Variety Show. He performed in front of the Queen and Prince Phillip the following year and has continued to

## 02

Diana's funeral in 1997, and performed at a tribute concert at the Althorp Estate in Northamptonshire for the late Princess the following year, as well as attending the event to mark the 10th anniversary of her death in 2007 alongside her sons and family.

Cliff was also a firm favourite of the late Queen Elizabeth II, and the monarch quipped to him that his knighthood for services to charity and music had been a "long time coming" during his 1995 investiture ceremony. Cliff has laughed over the years that he became so tongue tied that he spoke "gibberish" in response – though he also had a wry smile that the engraving on his medal's box read Knight Bachelor. He really would always be a Bachelor Boy!

The modest star said at the time he was proud that his work with his charitable trust had led to the accolade as he believed it meant the knighthood was "elevated" beyond his pop career, adding, "It's no great shakes, really, being a rock and roll singer." Cliff brought his three sisters to Buckingham Palace for the momentous occasion, having previously been accompanied by his mum to receive an OBE in 1980 – on that day, he officially changed his

02.    The newly knighted Sir Cliff Richard posed proudly alongside his sisters (L-R) Donna Gordon, Joan Pilgrim and Jacqui Harrison following his investiture at Buckingham Palace on 25th October 1995

Photo credit: Alamy

name by deed poll to Cliff Richard, to ensure the accolade was dished out in the name. But despite his joy at the occasion, he has spoken of his "anger" that his late dad Rodger was not there to share the moment with him. "He missed the best days of my life – he never saw the knighthood," Cliff told Piers Morgan. "When the Queen came to me with the sword I was a nervous wreck. When she tapped that on my shoulder, had my dad been there, it would have been fantastic. I'd have loved him to see that."

03. *He saw Queen Elizabeth II again a month after receiving his knighthood at the Royal Variety Performance on 20th November 1995*

*Photo credit:* Alamy

04. *A regular with the royals, he shook hands with Prince Charles at the Daily Mirror's Pride of Britain ceremony at the Grosvenor House Hotel, London on 31st October 2016*

*Photo credit:* Adam Gerrard/Daily Mirror

05. *Cliff was also friendly with Princess Diana, who chatted to tennis players Peter Fleming and Michael Chang along with Cliff and DJ Mike Read at Raynes Park, London on 19th June 1989*

*Photo credit:* Steve Wood/Daily Express

06. Cliff brought along his mum Dorothy to meet Princess Margaret and the Bishop of Bath at the Eton College Mission, Hackney Wick on 22nd March 1962

**Photo credit:** Tony Eyles/Daily Herald

07. He performed with Dame Vera Lynn and Harry Secombe at Buckingham Palace for World War II VE day 50th anniversary celebrations on 8th May 1995

**Photo credit:** Nicol/Daily Mirror

08. Queen Elizabeth II mingled on stage with Cliff, Sir Paul McCartney and Ricky Martin after they performed at her Golden Jubilee concert at Buckingham Palace on 3rd June 2002

Photo credit: Alamy

09. Riding an open top bus alongside Katherine Jenkins, Chris Eubank and Giles Terera along London's Pall Mall during the Queen's Platinum Pageant on 5th June 2022

Photo credit: Mirrorpix

10 Cliff performs in front of a sea of Union flags at Buckingham Palace for Queen Elizabeth II's Diamond Jubilee concert on 4th June 2012

**Photo credit:** Alamy

01

*Prayer has given strength to the star, performing here at the Royal Albert Hall on 18th October 2015, throughout turbulent times*

**Photo credit:** Neil Lupin/
Redferns/Getty

# SAVIOUR'S DAY:

## How Cliff's faith saved him

In 1988, the singer released one of his most famous Christmas songs, Mistletoe and Wine – but made sure he was first completely happy with its lyrics. He ensured Christianity featured in the meaning, without requesting writing royalties, explaining to Cross Rhythms: "The lyrics said 'snow, smoke, a smile and a joke,' I changed it to 'love and laughter, joy ever after, ours for the taking if you follow the Master'."

It was the biggest-selling song of the year, so two years later, he released another religious song at Christmas, and topped the charts once again with Saviour's Day. "Our nation was listening to Christian Christmas lyrics," he continued. "But it's very hard to do that, I don't expect to do that again".

He was certainly wrong about that! In 1999, he recorded The Lord's Prayer to the tune of Auld Lang Syne in the Millennium Prayer - a combination Cliff admitted at the time might make some listeners "want to puke". But personally, he felt it made the perfect Christmas single for the 2000th anniversary of Christ's birth, an element he felt was being forgotten at the millennium. The UK's biggest radio stations, including BBC Radio 2, refused to play the track – he had previously not been played on Virgin Radio's airwaves – yet the song still raced to No.1 where it stayed for three weeks, selling almost a million copies, and raising a million for the charity Children's Promise. Cliff's faith was now an integral part of his career, and getting stronger.

**If anything, I believe harder and more furiously now than I did before"**

133

His Christianity would play its most important role during the most difficult period of his life, in 2014, when police investigated historic claims of sexual assault, which he has always denied and the investigation was subsequently dropped due to a lack of evidence in 2016. The singer was never arrested or charged. Yet in that time, he endured the BBC broadcasting footage of his Berkshire home being searched, which he later successfully sued both the BBC and South Yorkshire Police over and received damages in compensation.

In the tumultuous time in between, Cliff's friends rallied in their support - he had thankfully been at home with close friends in Portugal when he first heard the search was due to take place, and they comforted him when he fell to the floor in tears. Cilla Black stated proudly she was sure the allegations against her "very close friend" were "without foundation", while Gloria Hunniford wrote a witness statement supporting him during his legal battle. Cliff also told Iain Dale in 2023 that pal Sir Elton John was one of the first people to call him during his legal challenge, telling him: "Take them by the throat." Along with radio host Paul Gambaccini he went on to campaign for a change in the law to prevent the media naming those accused of offences prior to charge.

Yet Cliff, who retreated to Barbados and Portugal, has since spoken candidly about how he relied on his faith during the darkest hours to get him through traumatic sleepless nights. He recalled to the Daily Mail: "God knew it was false. I used to comfort myself with that." He would spend his periods of insomnia praying for others, and even told God he had decided to forgive his accuser. In turn, his experience made his faith even stronger as he felt reliant on it in his lowest moments, adding: "If anything, I believe harder and more furiously now than I did before."

*02.* *Cliff's 1988 Christmas single Mistletoe and Wine is still a firm festive favourite*

02

03. The singer opened the *Tearcraft* shop in Newcastle on 4th February 1981 to raise money for the *TEAR Fund*, the International Christian charity he throws concerts in aid of

Photo credit: NCJ Archive

04. Cliff discussed his faith with the Rev John Wesson, Rector of St Martin in the Bull Ring, Birmingham, on 10th December 1987

Photo credit: Birmingham Post and Mail

05.   *Cliff celebrated the 25th anniversary of*
      *Christian charity TEAR Fund with a circle of*
      *"caring hands" on 7th January 1992*

**Photo credit:** Bill Kennedy/Daily Mirror

07

06.  He signed copies of his autobiography Single
     Minded, which explores his Christian faith, in
     September 1988

     Photo credit: John Downing/Daily Express

07.  The star has made regular appearances on
     the BBC's Songs of Praise TV Programme,
     including in October 1993

     Photo credit: Ian Bradshaw/Shutterstock

**08.** He performed his No. 1 hit Millennium Prayer on Songs of Praise at the Millennium Stadium in Cardiff, Wales on 2nd January 2000

**Photo credit:** Western Mail Archive

**09.** A huge crowd turned out in Cardiff to cheer on the star as the BBC series welcomed the new millennium

**Photo credit:** Western Mail Archive

10. By the end of the 1990s, Cliff was a staple soundtrack to Christmas, and posed by a tree in Birmingham on 14th December 1999

**Photo credit:** Mike Moore/Daily Mirror

11.  Along with radio host Paul
     Gambaccini, Daniel Janner QC and
     Michael Grade, Cliff campaigned
     for anonymity for those accused of
     offences prior to charge, appearing
     outside the Houses of Parliament on
     1st July 2019

Photo credit: Shutterstock

# CLIFF'S

# ARMY:
## His loyal fanbase

I t was obvious to Cliff from his teenage years that there would be one relationship he would prioritise throughout his life and career: his connection with his fans. It is a relationship that has stood the test of time as his fans still show him an unyielding loyalty seven decades later.

Though at the time it was his understanding that he needed to appear to be available to his audience, over the years many of his most dedicated supporters insisted they would have adored him regardless of his single status. He wrote a thank you song, Golden, to mark his 75th birthday describing his beloved supporters as "the treasure in my soul".

In 2003, fans camped for two weeks for the chance to buy tickets for his upcoming Royal Albert Hall gigs. By 2008, when Cliff announced his 2009 50th anniversary tour with The Shadows, local councils including in Sheffield had to intervene to stop his committed fanbase camping before the tickets went on sale for health and safety reasons, much to the fans' chagrin. At the time Viv Johnson, a 60-year-old grandmother who had previously spent a fortnight camping for tickets to see her idol, aired her disappointment, telling The Daily Telegraph:

"We're adults. We've never had any trouble and after a cup of tea we're asleep by 11pm." Alas, Cliff camp was no more.

Indeed, as his audience grew up from screaming adolescents to people with their own families, Cliff notes there is an added poignancy when he looks into his crowds and sees audience members sharing emotional moments together, with songs clearly representing personal meanings to them. He told Paul O'Grady: "Most singers who have survived a certain period of time, you find that you become other people's memories." He added that he often forgets his own lyrics, because he finds himself wondering what significance a track like Living Doll might have for the enamoured couples in front of him, and what it means to them. "Whatever it is, it's a huge memory for them, and I find that a privilege," he continued, with pride at having played a part in his fans' love and life stories.

He also spoke gratefully for the prayers and warm wishes he received from his fans during his most turbulent times, which went some way to helping reassure him that he was never alone at any point. His 2015 track, Golden contains lyrics about standing side by side and going through storms together.

02. By 1960, two dedicated Cliff fans Anita Croft and Janice Norman had collected nearly 2,000 photos of their idol, who they met backstage at the Coventry Theatre on 12th April 1960

**Photo credit:** Coventry Evening Telegraph

03. (L-R:) Sisters Susan and Sally Hoskins from Guildford, Surrey queued from 6am on 25th February 2001 for tickets to his Off The Record concert at the Royal Albert Hall

**Photo credit:** Jonathan Buckmaster/Daily Express

04. Fans flocked from all over the world for the Fabulous Rock 'N' Roll Tour, held at Lincoln Castle, on 24th June 2017

**Photo credit:** Anna Draper/Lincolnshire Echo

05. Even workers at the EMI factory in Hayes, Middlesex were fans, and he was mobbed and kissed when he turned up to collect his first gold disc for selling a million copies of Living Doll on 5th November 1959

**Photo credit:** Arthur Greated/Daily Mirror

06. Cliff's car journeys became a game of chase for excited school children. The singer had presented prizes at Sadler's Well Theatre in London on 6th October 1960

    Photo credit: Alisdair Macdonald/Daily Mirror

07. No Summer Holiday for Cliff! He was unable to attend his own premiere, when enthusiastic fans saw police forced to shut down Leicester Square on 10th January 1963

    Photo credit: Daily Mirror

08. One fan, Barbara Crockett, won a competition to meet her favourite star - and presented him with a handmade jumper at his Hammersmith Odeon concert on 25th November 1981

    Photo credit: Birmingham Post and Mail

09. Cliff was joined by fans at the Birmingham NEC when he turned up to announce details of future concerts on 13th June 1990

Photo credit: Alan Williams/Birmingham Post and Mail

10. He's our bag! One fan shows off her Cliff accessory at the Fabulous Rock 'N' Roll Tour at Lincoln Castle on 24th June 2017

Photo credit: Anna Draper/Lincolnshire Echo

Long live The King! In the 1950s, young Harry Webb was inspired to become a rock 'n' roll singer by his idol, Elvis Presley - and copied his famous quiff

**Photo credit:** Mirrorpix

# CLIFF BY THE DECADES

His famously youthful looks have continued into his 85th year, and the Peter Pan of Pop certainly looks in great shape to continue playing tennis for another decade and a half.

From a teenage Elvis-obsessive, to becoming a multi-faceted showbusiness entertainer and now legendary British superstar still commanding the stage, take a look at Cliff Richard through the decades...

02.  The 1960s saw the hip-shaking rock 'n' roll
     star become music's most famous Christian,
     and in 1967 Cliff strove to strike a balance
     between the two important areas of his life

     Photo credit: Tom King/Daily Mirror

03.  Never one to shy away from a challenge,
     the 1970s saw Cliff set off for Luxembourg
     for a second crack at representing the UK at
     Eurovision on 4th April 1973

     Photo credit: Dennis Stone/Daily Mirror

05. In the 1990s Cliff purchased a Portugeuse farm, but continued entertaining throughout its vast renovations. He is pictured in London's Docklands Arena on 24th September 1992

Photo credit: Marcus Queenborough/ Birmingham Post and Mail

06. He maintained his home in Weybridge, Surrey for two decades, seen here in its extensive grounds on 21st September 2004, before downsizing to Berkshire in 2006

Photo credit: Mark Kehoe/Sunday Express

07.    *Gold standard: Cliff toured throughout
       the 2010s, spent 2015 celebrating his 75th
       birthday, followed by his Fabulous Rock 'N'
       Roll Tour at Lincoln Castle on 24th June 2017*

08.    *Still going strong into the 2020s, Cliff
       celebrated the 100th anniversary of
       Centre Court at the Wimbledon tennis
       championships on 30th June 2022*

**Photo credit:** Anna Draper/Lincolnshire Echo

**Photo credit:** Tim Merry/Daily Star